8629

SIGHTSEERS
ESSENTIAL TRAVEL GUIDES TO THE PAST

VIKING WORLD

A GUIDE TO 11th CENTURY SCANDINAVIA

JULIE FERRIS

KINGfISHER

KINGFISHER
Kingfisher Publications Plc
New Penderel House,
283–288 High Holborn,
London WC1V 7HZ

Written and edited by Julie Ferris and Sheila Clewley
Designer Veneta Altham

Illustrations John James
Kevin Maddison

Consultant Robin Allan
Researcher Prue Grice
DTP Co-ordinator Nicky Studdart
Production Controllers Jacquie Horner
Caroline Jackson
Picture Research Manager Jane Lambert
Indexer Sheila Clewley

First published by Kingfisher Publications Plc 2000
1 3 5 7 9 10 8 6 4 2

1TR/0500/WKT/ATLS/140MA

A CIP catalogue record for this book is available from
the British Library.

ISBN 0 7534 0413 3

Printed in
Hong Kong/China

Contents

The Viking world

Situated in the northernmost reaches of Europe is one of the most exciting tourist destinations. The Viking world is a land of hardy, courageous tribes living on farms or in fortified trading communities. The climate can be harsh and the winters long, but the customs and lifestyles of these extraordinary people who have a passion for trading and raiding are fascinating. Viking lands are ripe for discovery!

Sightseers' tip A Viking holiday is not for the squeamish. Warfare and fighting are very much part of their culture, and the traditional Norse religion involves animal and, at times, human sacrifice.

Hedeby, a large trading town in Viking Denmark, makes an ideal base for exploration. The town is well fortified with 10-metre high ramparts on three sides. Accommodation in town houses and on nearby farms is readily available

The first Viking raid was on Lindisfarne, Scotland, in 793. The Vikings plundered the monastery, stealing treasures.

Viking explorers reached Russia in the 850s. It is a land rich in goods which the Vikings can trade.

The year 874 saw the first Viki settlement established in Iceland It is an inhospitable land and life was hard for the pioneers.

Viking lands span huge areas so visitors must be prepared to travel a long way.

The three principal Viking trading centres are Ribe, Birka and Hedeby.

Most parts of the Viking world are ruled by wealthy and powerful kings.

The sparsely distributed population divides into three distinct groups – Swedes, Norwegians and Danes. However, they all speak the same language and have very similar customs. Vikings are great seafarers, and their adventuring has taken them as far afield as Greenland, America and the coast of North Africa.

Ship burials are a common sight in the Viking world. These graves are often marked out by stones in the shape of a boat, indicating that death is seen as a voyage into the unknown.

n 907, the Vikings attacked the wealthy city of Constantinople. However, they failed to capture it.

Viking Leif Eriksson explored Vinland in North America in c.1000 and established a Viking settlement.

By 1000, Christianity had spread far in the Viking world and became the official religion in Iceland.

5

Travelling around

If you are prone to seasickness then the Viking world is probably not the ideal holiday destination! Inland roads are little more than rough, muddy tracks, so Vikings travel everywhere they can by boat. Fortunately, their ships are the best in Europe. They are sturdy enough to cross oceans, and have flat bases so they can sail along shallow rivers.

Viking boats, or longships, are sometimes referred to as "serpents of the sea". This is because their prows are often decorated with a carving of a monstrous creature. Vikings believe that the monster will frighten enemy gods.

The frightening carved figureheads are removed from ship prows when sailing in friendly waters so that local gods are not upset.

Navigation is a problem on long voyages. Sailors have to rely on the sun and stars to work out their position at sea. They use wooden tools to measure the height of the sun.

Sightseers' tip   Most Viking settlements are situated near to water, and traders can often be seen unloading goods on the shore. Look out for newly arrived trading vessels if you are after holiday souvenirs.

In the winter, iron spikes are nailed into horses' hooves so they can grip the ice.

Long sea voyages are undertaken only in the summer months.

The amazing 37m Norwegian longship *Long Serpent* has room for 68 rowers.

If you need to travel overland you can walk, ride on horseback, or hitch a lift on a merchant's wagon. There are trackways between trading centres, but most are unsurfaced. Inland travel is much easier in the winter when the mud freezes over, and skates, skis and sledges can be used when the ground is covered in snow.

Skating is a great way to cross Scandinavia's frozen lakes and rivers. Skates are made from horse, ox or deer bone which is smoothed flat on the underside. Skis are handy for getting about in the snow. It may take a while to get your balance, but they are great fun!

Longships can reach a speed of 27 kilometres an hour under sail in a good wind. When powered by oars, the top speed is 11 kilometres an hour.

What to wear

Viking clothes are simple, yet practical. Men wear linen undershirts, belted woollen tunics and trousers, while women wear long, loose dresses and full-length aprons which they fasten with brooches. Vegetable dyes, decorative borders and embroidery are used to brighten the hard-wearing clothes. The weather is often bad, so don't forget to pack a warm wool or fur cloak.

Married Viking women cover their hair with a scarf as a sign of modesty.

The Vikings love jewellery and are famous for their beautiful gold, silver and bronze bracelets, necklaces and brooches.

Both men and women adorn themselves with items of jewellery, and you will be able to buy armrings, bracelets, necklaces, brooches and rings from local craftsmen. There should be something to suit every budget – from intricately decorated gold rings to simple bronze brooches.

Sightseers' tip

Female visitors will find the oval brooches used to fasten aprons very handy. Viking women hang useful items from them such as sewing tools, combs, purses and keys.

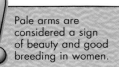
Pale arms are considered a sign of beauty and good breeding in women.

Look out for amber jewellery. Manufacture of it is an important industry in Hedeby.

Vikings use bear, seal and squirrel furs to make warm cloaks for the cold winters.

Cloaks are fastened using a brooch. If you are right-handed, make sure you fasten your cloak on your right shoulder so that your sword arm is not restricted by the heavy material.

Most Viking women weave their own fabric and make clothes for themselves and their families. Their sewing implements are usually made from wood or bone. If you are staying in a large trading town such as Hedeby in Viking Denmark, you may be able to buy silk from Asian merchants. Silk is very fashionable but extremely expensive.

Women wear their long hair tied in a knot at the back. Beards or drooping moustaches are a must for men. They are kept trim and tidy, and beards are even plaited by the fashion-conscious.

Both men and women wear slip-on leather shoes. They are often made from goatskin or cattle hide. The most popular style is a low-cut shoe, but ankle-length or taller boots are also available for men. The soles have no heels, and when they are worn out they can easily be replaced with new ones.

Food and drink

When it comes to food and drink, Viking families are very self-sufficient. Their farms and cattle provide them with corn, vegetables and meat. The rivers and seas yield a wonderful variety of fresh fish. Food is usually plentiful, particularly in the summer months, so you should eat well during your stay.

Sightseers' tip

Vikings eat twice a day – in the morning and in the evening. The meals are substantial and you will usually be offered more than one course.

Although tables and stools are often set up at mealtimes, Vikings sometimes opt for simply eating off their laps. They cut food with knives and eat with their fingers from wooden bowls and plates.

Vikings wash their food down with copious quantities of home-made beer.

Meat and fish are smoked or salted in the summer to provide food in the winter.

Vegetarians beware! Meat is the main part of the Viking diet. It is stewed or roasted.

Why not join a hunting party and catch your own dinner? As well as hunting wild boar and reindeer, Vikings take to the seas to hunt large sea mammals such as seals, whales and walruses.

All cooking is done by the women of the household. They use a large metal cauldron suspended over the fire by a chain fixed to the roof of the longhouse (a Viking home).

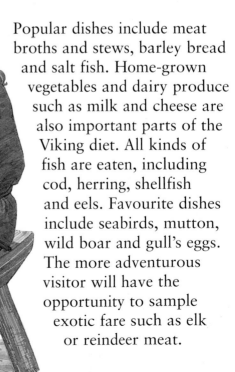

Popular dishes include meat broths and stews, barley bread and salt fish. Home-grown vegetables and dairy produce such as milk and cheese are also important parts of the Viking diet. All kinds of fish are eaten, including cod, herring, shellfish and eels. Favourite dishes include seabirds, mutton, wild boar and gull's eggs. The more adventurous visitor will have the opportunity to sample exotic fare such as elk or reindeer meat.

Shopping

Although best known for their daring summer raids, the Vikings are equally impressive as traders. They have established extensive trading routes all over Europe, and their merchants sell goods such as timber, amber and animal furs. Hedeby is a bustling trading town where you will be able to buy goods from foreign lands, as well as local produce.

Traditionally, merchants used the barter system (exchanged goods of equal value), but payment in coins is now more common. Coins minted in Hedeby feature a Viking ship.

The town has crowded streets lined with craftsmen's houses and stalls offering a diverse range of goods. It is the perfect place to pick up holiday souvenirs. You could buy cloth from a weaver, a comb from an antler-carver, a sword from a blacksmith, or silks and spices from eastern merchants.

The town of Hedeby also has a flourishing slave market. People are captured on raids and sold as slaves throughout the Viking world.

Most important towns mint their own coins, usually made of silver.

Piracy is common, so trading towns are well-defended and have look-outs.

A town market is the perfect place to buy fresh food from local farms.

Blacksmiths are very important craftsmen. As well as repairing tools and weapons, they make a wide variety of iron goods including swords, pots, pans and keys.

Different parts of the Viking world are famed for trading in particular goods. The Norwegians supply timber, Greenland and Iceland trade in seal oil and woollens, and iron ore comes from Sweden. The Vikings also import wine from France, slaves and fur from Russia, and silk and spices from Constantinople and Persia. Goods are transported by sea or overland by river.

Sightseers' tip
As you explore the busy market streets, you will notice that many craftsmen work outside. This is because Viking houses let in very little daylight.

Accommodation

Vikings are very hospitable so you should have no trouble finding somewhere to stay. A farm on the outskirts of town would make a perfect holiday base. Called longhouses, Viking homes consist of an enormous room where the entire family, guests, servants and slaves eat, work and sleep.

Longhouses usually don't have windows. This is because a warm house is considered more important than a well-lit one!

If you prefer to stay in the town centre, you should be able to find accommodation in a town house. However, they are much smaller than longhouses.

The sides of a Viking longhouse are lined with earth platforms where people sleep. There is very little furniture. Most homes have a table, a few low stools, and lockable, wooden chests to store belongings.

Women spend a lot of time in the longhouse. As well as looking after the children, they prepare and cook the food, weave cloth and make clothes for the family.

Vikings are famed for their hospitality and for opening their homes to strangers.

A cosy longhouse will provide welcome shelter from the cold weather.

It is harder to find accommodation during religious festivals.

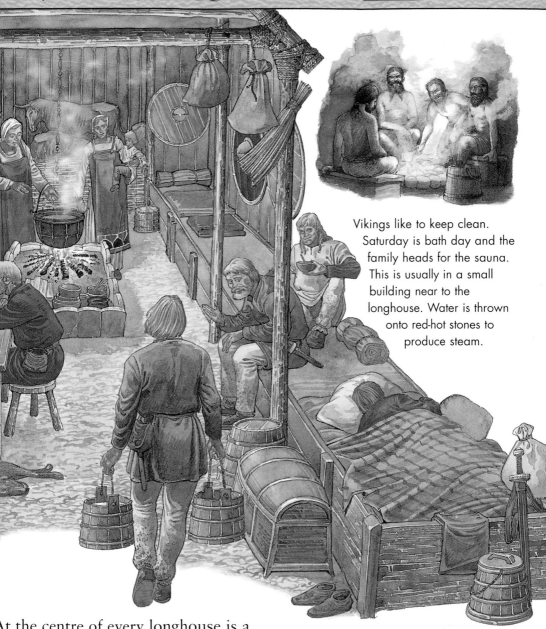

Vikings like to keep clean. Saturday is bath day and the family heads for the sauna. This is usually in a small building near to the longhouse. Water is thrown onto red-hot stones to produce steam.

At the centre of every longhouse is a huge fireplace edged with stones. It is a vital source of heat and is used for cooking food. However, there is no chimney, so smoke must escape through a small hole in the roof.

Sightseers' tip

To maximize space in the longhouse, bedding is rolled up during the day. Important household members sleep nearest to the fire, where it is warm.

15

A Viking raid

Sightseers' tip There are strict rules about what weapons you can take on a raid, but these vary from area to area. You will be allocated a chest on the longship in which you can store your gear. The chest also makes a useful seat for when you take your turn rowing.

For the ultimate Viking experience, make sure you join a raiding party. The raids are organized by local lords (jarls) and the most popular targets are the treasure-filled monasteries of England, Ireland and France. Longships depart from coastal Viking towns in the spring and summer months, and you should have no trouble finding a boat to take you – there are up to 60 longships on an average raid.

The most feared warriors are called "berserks". They never wear armour.

Most monasteries and towns are unguarded, so it is easy for Vikings to plunder treasure.

Fight with the sun behind you so that your opponent will be dazzled by it.

Raids are not for the faint-hearted. The surprise attacks can be very violent and bloody – anyone who resists the Vikings in their search for treasures to steal is killed. Viking boys are trained to fight from a very young age. They practise fighting with blunt, wooden weapons, and are only allowed to use a proper weapon when they become an adult.

Longships are also used for sea battles. After firing arrows and throwing spears at an enemy ship, the longships draw close and hand-to-hand fighting begins.

Protective clothing is vital. If you can't afford a chain-mail shirt, make sure you invest in a padded leather tunic. An iron helmet and a wooden shield are a must.

Axes and spears are popular weapons, but double-edged swords are prized above all. They are passed down from father to son and are given nicknames such as "mail-biter".

17

A Viking feast

For the best in Viking entertainment, make sure you attend a feast. They are organized by local jarls and, as well as being great fun, are perfect for exchanging news and gossip and doing business. The jarl's great hall is lined with benches, the finest tableware is brought out and the best of Viking cuisine is served. However, the most important thing at any feast is drinking – they can get very rowdy!

Make sure you dress in your finest clothes and most expensive jewellery. It is important to look your best at a feast as the most important local Vikings are sure to be there.

Sightseers' tip

A feast can las for several days – the longer it lasts the more the jarl's reputatio for generosity is enhanced. The best time for feasting is i the winter, after the harvest. Jarls who want to impress host a lavish feast in mid-winter, when food is scarce.

Servants will regularly refill your drinking horn – and you will have to drink it all! If you put the horn down it will fall over, so it has to be empty first.

Seating arrangements at a feast are often hierarchical – important guests have the honour of sitting next to the jarl. Occasionally, seating is decided by drawing lots.

Women can serve food and drink, but must leave if things get too rowdy.

Feasts are often held on important religious days when sacrifices are also made.

You may have to take a turn at reciting a verse, but don't worry, you can make it up!

Guests at a feast can get very boisterous, so it is common for entertainers to open with a call for silence. Poems are recited that usually include a couple of verses praising the host.

Professional poets (skalds) are hired to entertain guests. Their poems are about famous battles or events in Viking history. Poems are passed from generation to generation, but have not been written down. Viking verse is famed for its descriptions of everyday things – a battle is a 'game of iron' and a 'speech servant' is a tongue.

Leisure time

Vikings are hard workers and do not have a great deal of spare time. What free time they have is often spent perfecting fighting techniques – warrior skills are very important to them. In fact, most leisure activities on offer involve fighting. A holiday in the Viking world is not for the faint-hearted!

Sightseers' tip Vikings love to gamble. They place bets on the outcome of spectator sports such as horse fighting and wrestling.

A favourite spectator sport is horse fighting. Two stallions battle together, egged on by their owners who beat them with sticks to make them fight more viciously.

Wrestling, juggling with knives and fencing are all dangerous sports enjoyed by Vikings. Even swimming competitions can be bloodthirsty. They are not won by outswimming an opponent – instead you must try to drown other competitors!

The Vikings do enjoy some quieter, less violen forms of entertainment. Board games are very popular, and the most widely played is hnefataf It is a game of strategy, similar to chess.

Skiing is a popular leisure activity as well as an effective way to get around.

Inventing riddles and swapping insults are considered great fun by the Vikings.

Look out for home-made, finely carved games pieces. They make lovely souvenirs.

Wrestling contests take place in the open air. Spectators gather round the fighters, standing close so that they can get a good view of the fighting action.

Vikings are very competitive in sports. Winning is a matter of honour, and sportsmen will stop at nothing to be victorious. In fact, it is not unusual for a wrestling contest to end in serious injury, or even the death of one of the opponents. The Vikings really do enjoy bloodthirsty spectacles!

21

Temple of Uppsala

Vikings are very tolerant when it comes to religion. Their own Norse religion involves the worship of many gods, although the three main ones are Odin (the god of war and wisdom), Thor (the god of thunder) and Frey (the god of nature and fertility). Increasingly, however, Vikings are converting to Christianity.

New Christian churches are being built all over the Viking world. Called "stave" churches, they are made of wood and have tall, triangular roof

Sightseers' tip According to Norse religion, if a Viking dies in battle he is taken to Valhalla (the god Odin's great hall), where he feasts and drinks forever.

Christian burials are increasingly the norm, but you may witness a traditional chief's funeral. The chief's body is placed on a boat, which is then set alight.

Although Norse worship normally takes place in the open air, there is a famous temple at Uppsala in Sweden that is definitely worth a visit. The temple houses huge statues of Odin, Thor and Frey, and every nine years a special festival is held there. A sacrifice is made of nine males of every living thing, from dogs and horses to human beings. The heads are offered to the gods, and the bodies are hung in a sacred grove.

There are no priests in Norse religion. Instead, local chiefs lead worship and make sacrifices.

Ritual feasts are often held in which a sacrificial animal is killed and eaten.

You will see beautiful carved statues of gods all over the Viking world.

Norse worship often takes place at natural landmarks such as lakes or groves.

Many of the poems you will hear at feasts are about the Norse gods and their adventures.

Exploring north

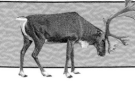

If you are planning a long stay in Viking lands, why not visit one of the northern colonies? Iceland was first settled in 874 and is now a well-established community with a large population. Greenland was discovered in the 980s by Erik the Red, a Viking who was outlawed from Iceland for manslaughter. It is a cold, barren place, but was named Greenland to entice other Vikings to move there!

Longhouses in Iceland and Greenland are covered with peat and slightly sunk in the ground to protect against the cold.

Vikings have settled in only the most habitable parts of Iceland and Greenland. As well as tending to their crops and livestock, they trade regularly with other parts of the Viking world. They export furs and hides, ropes, oil and falcons, and import corn, iron and timber. Timber is a necessary import as few trees grow in the extreme climate.

The only way to reach Iceland, Greenland and Vinland is by boat.

Make sure you wear warm furs – it can be very cold in the northern colonies.

A lawspeaker is elected every three years to recite the law at the Althing.

If you are feeling very adventurous, you could travel west to the newest Viking settlement. Vinland was discovered by Leif Eriksson, and has a good climate and fertile land. However, its distance and the resistance of the natives put into doubt the future of this colony.

Greenland has periods of continuous sun in the summer and continuous dark in the winter. This is because it is so far north.

If you visit Iceland in the summer, make sure you attend the Althing. At this assembly laws are agreed, important issues discussed, disputes settled and gossip exchanged. There is also a huge fair, so it's great for buying souvenirs!

Sightseers' tip
"Things" are held all over the Viking world, but these mostly deal with local issues and disputes. The Althing, however, is more like a national assembly.

Eastern trade routes

The Vikings have established extensive trade routes and settlements eastwards and southwards through the land of the Slavs (Russia). Joining a trading expedition is a great way to see at first hand the full extent of the Viking world and its neighbours. You could even visit Constantinople, the largest city in the world.

Vikings travel by boat along the vast network of rivers. When they need to change river or are forced to travel overland to avoid rapids, they use logs to roll the boat over the ground.

The native Slavs call the Vikings who trade and settle in their land "Rus", and the area is increasingly referred to as Russia. The largest settlements are at Novgorod and Kiev.

The eastern trade routes are a must for serious souvenir hunters! You will be able to buy everything from furs and silk to spices and slaves.

The Rus are so mistrustful of each other that they will not leave the house without an armed escort.

The Rus do not cultivate their own land. Instead, food is obtained from the land of the Slavs.

Because of previous raids, Viking numbers are restricted in Constantinople.

The eastern trade routes eventually lead to Constantinople – capital city of the Byzantine empire (the eastern half of the old Roman empire). The Vikings call it Miklagard, which means "the great city". It is a huge trading centre, with a population of a million people.

Sightseers' tip Constantinople is a beautiful city, famed for its fine churches and palaces. The emperor's court is renowned throughout the world for its elegance and wealth.

27

Survival guide

A visit to Viking lands is not for the fearful traveller. Life for the Vikings is tough and demanding – they work hard and play even harder. However, the adventurous and thrill-seeking globetrotter will find the customs and way of life of these northern people both challenging and fascinating.

Health

Viking life expectancy can be as high as 55 years. They are quite a healthy race, although they do suffer from lice and fleas, and stomach disorders are common. Stomach aches are probably caused by traces of poisonous weeds which are often found in the bread grain. Don't worry too much about this – if you do succumb, the discomfort will soon pass.

Battle-wounded warriors are fed an onion and herb porridge. If the wound develops an onion odour, it is concluded that the intestine has been pierced by a sword and that the victim will die.

Administration

Rune stones are placed to claim ownership of a patch of land, or to commemorate a deceased friend or relative. The alphabet is made chiefly of straight lines. This makes carving inscriptions on wood or stone relatively easy.

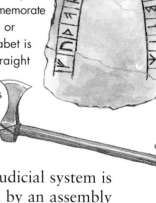

The Viking judicial system is administered by an assembly known as the thing. This gathering of local land owners can last for weeks at a time. The thing discusses local problems and settles arguments about theft, murder and land ownership.

The thing can be a social occasion as well as a judicial forum.

A duel can be fascinating to watch. But stand well back!

Rune stones are often beautifully decorated with elaborate patterns.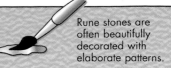

aw and order

tay on the right side of the law during your isit! Strict rules and customs protect Vikings nd their property, and there are swift and arsh punishments for anyone caught reaking these laws. A thief, for nstance, can expect to be hanged, nd a suspected witch will die orribly through stoning, rowning or being sunk n a bog.

Disagreements are often settled by duel. Opponents face one another on a small area of land marked out by a cloth. Swords and axes are favourite weapons, and a shield is essential for defence. Duels are usually fought to the death.

❓ Souvenir quiz

Take your time exploring the Viking World. It is a fascinating place with plenty to see and experience. Before you leave, test your knowledge with this fun quiz. You will find the answers on page 32.

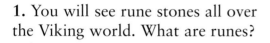

1. You will see rune stones all over the Viking world. What are runes?

a) They are drawings of Vikings in battle

b) They are letters in the Viking alphabet

c) They are sign posts

2. Why are meat and fish salted during the summer months?

a) To preserve them so that they can be eaten during the winter

b) To improve flavour – Vikings like salty food

c) To make them more tender

3. What is a "berserk"?

a) A type of bear

b) A stew made with gulls' eggs

c) A particularly fierce warrior

4. Why do you have to empty your drinking horn before putting it down?

a) Because it does not have a flat bottom, so the drink will spill out

b) To show politeness – it is rude not to finish your drink

c) So you will be served some more

5. If you hear a Viking use the expression "speech servant", what is he talking about?

a) A slave who recites poetry and folklore

b) A servant whose tongue has been removed to stop him gossiping

c) It is the poetic term for the tongue

What is a "jarl"?

It is a type of cheese particularly popular in Iceland

It is the term used to describe a local lord

It is a cooking pot used for making soup

Of what is Frey the Norse god?

Frey is the god of war

Frey is the god of wine and beer

Frey is the god of nature and fertility

What is "hnefatafl"?

It is a board game similar to chess

It is a club carried by the god Odin

It is a wooden storage chest

9. Why was Erik the Red, the Viking discoverer of Greenland, outlawed from Iceland?

a) He was accused of stealing sheep from a neighbouring farm

b) He scrawled runic graffiti all over the local lord's longhouse

c) He committed manslaughter

10. Who discovered Vinland?

a) Leif Eriksson

b) Erik the Red

c) Vik the Viking

11. Why do Viking women cover their hair with a scarf?

a) As a sign of modesty

b) To keep their hair tidy and out of their eyes

c) To keep their heads warm in the cold winter months

Index

Acknowledgements

The consultant
Robin Allan is a senior lecturer in the Scandinavian Studies department of University College London.

Additional design
Mike Davis, Jane Tassie

Picture credits
b = bottom, c = centre, l = left, r = right, t = top
p.6tl The Bridgeman Art Library/University of Oslo, Norway;

p.8cl The Bridgeman Art Library/Nationalmuseet, Copenhagen, Denmark; p.12tr Werner Forman Archive/Statens Historiska Museum, Stockholm; p.17bc Werner Forman Archive/Statens Historiska Museum, Stockholm; p. 18bl Ancient Art & Architecture

Every effort has been made to trace the copyright holders of the photographs. The publishers apologise for any inconvenience caused.

Souvenir quiz answers

This book is set in the year 1010.

1 = b) 2 = a) 3 = c) 4 = a) 5 = c) 6 = b) 7 = c) 8 = a) 9 = c) 10 = a) 11 = a)